SLIME SCIENCE

Test It Out!

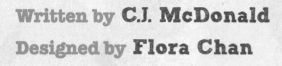

Written by **C.J. McDonald**
Designed by **Flora Chan**

an imprint of
SCHOLASTIC
scholastic.com

10 9 8 7 6 5 4 3 2 1
ISBN: 978-1-338-79692-6
Printed in Guangzhou, China
5053487 09/21
Photos ©: 6 bottom right: IanDagnall Computing/Alamy; 40 bottom left: Elvira Galimova/Getty Images; 41: Pomah/ Dreamstime. All other photos © Scholastic Inc. and Shuttsrstock.com.

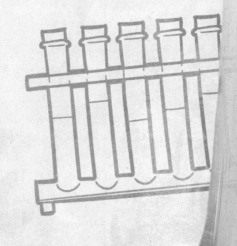

TABLE OF CONTENTS

SLIME-OLOGY 101

There are books for English class, math class, and social studies, but this book is about *the really gross science of slime.* We're talking hours of *squishy, oozing, disgusting fun.* So be prepared, because . . .

IT'S SLIME TIME!

Slime science is about being a **mad scientist**. It's about squeezing away stress. It's about **awesome prank opportunities**. It's sloppy, blobby bliss.

Before we *get gooing*, let's address some important safety tips. And we promise to make it fun.

NOW, PAY ATTENTION, OKAY?

SLIME SAFETY

Let's cover a few basic rules, because even slime comes with a few.

DO:

- Keep an adult partner in slime nearby when making or working with slime.
- Cover the work area with paper to prevent messes. The paper can double as a place to take notes.
- Follow all instructions in order for best results. **No slime crimes here**.
- Use only the ingredients listed.
- Keep slime off carpet, clothing, furniture, toys, pets, brothers and sisters, and alien life forms.
- Use white vinegar to clean up slimy messes.
- **Store slime in covered containers or resealable bags**. In hotter months or in hotter places, store it in the fridge.
- Clean up after all experiments.
- Wash hands after all experiments or after handling slime.
- In case of contact with eyes, rinse with plenty of water and seek medical advice. If any of the experiments are swallowed, seek medical advice right away. Take the ingredients with you.

DON'T EVEN THINK ABOUT IT:

- NO eating slime.
- NO feeding slime to a friend, a brother, or a sister.
- And **NO feeding it to anyone at all**. That includes pets—and worst enemies.
- NO disposing of slime down the sink. It belongs in the trash and **only in the trash**.
- NO putting chemicals in and near the mouth, eyes, ears, or nose.

THE WEIRD AND WONDERFUL WORLD OF SLIME SCIENCE

Okay, so maybe this is obvious, but maybe not. This is how scientific observation works. When water pours, ketchup squirts, or maple syrup flows over your waffles, those liquids pour a little differently. **That's because they differ in viscosity.**

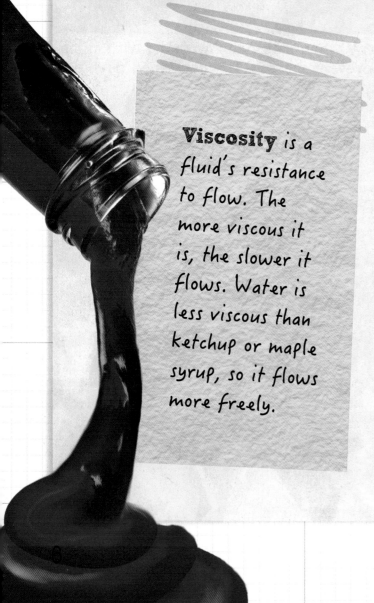

Viscosity is a fluid's resistance to flow. The more viscous it is, the slower it flows. Water is less viscous than ketchup or maple syrup, so it flows more freely.

Water, oil, and alcohol are called **Newtonian fluids**, named for the freaky-smart scientist Sir Isaac Newton. He found temperature affects the viscosity of fluids.

Try It!
with the slime that came with
this book. Does it feel solid when
squeezed? Does it **OOZE**?

Slime is called a **non-Newtonian fluid**.
Temperature doesn't change its viscosity.
Stress does—stress as in . . . squishing,
squeezing, and stirring.

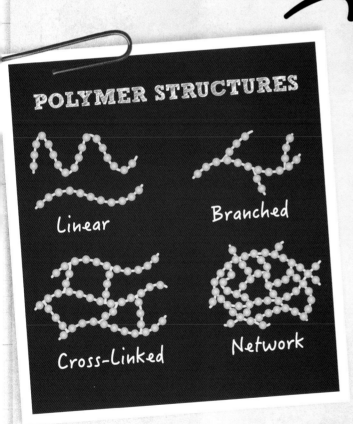

POLYMER STRUCTURES

Linear

Branched

Cross-Linked

Network

Slime gets its superpowers
from polymers. *Poly* means
"many." In this case, many
refers to slime's many
repeating molecules linked
together in an X-shaped chain.
The chainlike bonds allow
slime to be pulled or squished
without breaking.

But not all polymers are alike.
Each has its own chemical
makeup. That unique makeup
affects how slippery, slimy, or
stretchy the slime is. And now,

IT'S SLIME TIME!

BLUE OOZE

Some things don't go together—**purple** and orange, cats and dogs, or maybe broccoli with anything. Oil and water are like that. What happens when we mix them? Let's find out!

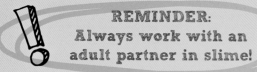 **What You Need**

☐ Clean jelly jar with lid
☐ Blue food coloring
☐ Spoon or craft stick
☐ Vegetable oil
☐ Tape
☐ Water

REMINDER:
Always work with an adult partner in slime!

How to Do It

1. Fill jar halfway with water.

2. Stir a few drops of food coloring into the water.

3. Slowly fill the rest of the jar with oil, and watch carefully. The oil just sits there on top of the water. They're not mixing together.

4. Put the lid on the jar, and seal the lid by wrapping tape all around the bottom of it.

5. Gently turn the jar upside down. Watch the water become a **big blue blob!**

6. Holding the jar over a sink (just to be extra safe), shake it hard a few times. The big blue blob should become a bunch of smaller blobs!

7. Turn the jar up and down fast for about ten seconds. Now you should have bunches and bunches of mini blobs!

Time for Slime-Sci

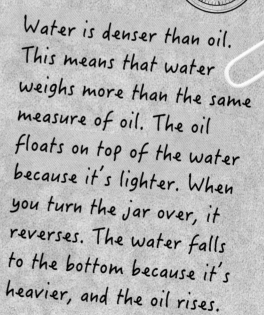

Water is denser than oil. This means that water weighs more than the same measure of oil. The oil floats on top of the water because it's lighter. When you turn the jar over, it reverses. The water falls to the bottom because it's heavier, and the oil rises.

OOZING DROPS

To achieve some ooze, it's time to pay some dues with patience—but it will be worth it!

☑ What You Need

- ☐ Tall clear jar
- ☐ Ice cube tray
- ☐ Water
- ☐ Food coloring
- ☐ Vegetable oil
- ☐ Funnel

How to Do It

1. Fill the ice cube tray with water. Add a drop or two of food coloring into one of the wells, and put the tray into the freezer until the water hardens. *Now be patient!*

2. Fill the jar about halfway with oil.

10

3. Set the small end of the funnel over the mouth of the jar.

4. Remove the ice from the freezer. Set the colored ice cube in the funnel with the open end pointing down.

5. Watch what happens as the colored water melts. Colorful blobs drip from the funnel into the oil as **smaller blobs ooze around on the bottom of the jar.**

6. For faster results (if there's no time for that patience thing), skip the first step, and use a dropper to squeeze colored water into the oil. The results will be slightly less cool but faster.

Time for Slime-Sci

Just as we learned in our first experiment, water is denser than oil. Its density sends droplets to the bottom of the jar. Hydrogen bonds within the water give the droplets their perfectly round shape.

MAGNETIC SLIME

This slithery, sliding marvel of magnetism will amaze friends and family!

☑ What You Need

- ☐ 2 tbsp. (29.6 ml) white glue
- ☐ 1 tbsp. (12.8 g) iron oxide powder (available at department stores or online)
- ☐ 2 tbsp. (29.6 ml) liquid starch
- ☐ Disposable cup
- ☐ Neodymium magnet (available at craft or home supply stores)

- ☐ Tablespoon
- ☐ Craft stick
- ☐ Paper towels
- ☐ Disposable gloves

How to Do It

1. Put 1 tbsp. (12.8 g) of iron oxide powder in your disposable cup.

2. Stir in 2 tbsp. (29.6 ml) of liquid starch.

3. Then 2 tbsp. (29.6 ml) of white glue.

4. Stir until all ingredients are completely mixed, and the slime texture is the same throughout.

5. Put on your gloves.

6. Once your slime is sticky, remove it from the cup.

7. Squeeze it like bread dough until it dries. If needed, use a paper towel to help dab off moisture.

8. Once it's dry, remove gloves and handle the slime with bare hands.

9. Now use the magnet to make the slime slither and slide. *It's alive!!!*

Keep magnets away from younger children and pets and from electronics, such as phones, tablets, and computers!

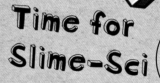

Time for Slime-Sci

Glue, a polymer that contains long molecules of polyvinyl acetate, gives this slime its sticky superpowers. Iron oxide contains the mineral magnetite, which is seriously magnetic.

13

ACUPUNCTURE

It's time to see polymers work in an unexpected way. And don't worry. This kind of acupuncture doesn't use needles.

How to Do It

1. Fill the bag about halfway with tap water. Add red food coloring until the water looks like blood. (We can pretend, can't we?) Seal the bag.

14

2. Using the help of an adult partner in slime, hold the bag over the sink. Then twist a pencil through one side of the bag and out the other side. The bag has two holes in it, but **it isn't bleeding**!

3. Do the same thing with the other pencils. *Still no bleeding*!

Time for Slime-Sci

The polymers aren't found in the blood-colored water. They're found in the bag itself. When pencils poke through the bag, the water doesn't leak because the long molecules in the bag's polymers close tightly around each pencil as it passes through.

15

HEAVING MILK

Some people or things are an instant recipe for drama. Well, let's create a little drama of our own with things that just don't mix!

☑ **What You Need**

☐ A pie plate or cake pan
☐ Whole milk
☐ Food coloring
☐ Dishwashing liquid

How to Do It

1. Pour milk into the pie plate or cake pan.

2. Put a drop of food coloring into the milk.

3. Put a drop of dishwashing liquid on top of the food coloring. The food coloring will swirl around madly as the milk begins to **ooze**!

4. For even more fun, put several drops of food coloring of different colors in separate areas throughout the plate or pan. Put a drop of dishwashing liquid on each drop, and watch as a **rainbow** of swirling colors appears!

Time for Slime-Sci

Whole milk contains both water and fat. We've already learned water and fat don't mix. But the water and fat in the milk and food coloring make millions of rapid connections with the detergent. This causes the wonderfully bizarre boiling effect.

GLOW-IN-THE-DARK SLIME

This spooky goo will be the light of the party. Prepare to be blinded by slime science!

☑ What You Need

- ☐ 2 cups (240 g) cornstarch
- ☐ 1-2 cups (237-474 ml) tonic water with quinine
- ☐ Mixing bowl
- ☐ Mixing spoon
- ☐ UV black light (available in department or home supply stores)

How to Do It

1. Pour the cornstarch into a bowl.

2. Add 1 cup (237 ml) of tonic water. Stir to combine. Add more tonic water if the slime is too thick.

3. Turn off the lights, and shine the UV black light on your slime. Is it science or magic—or maybe a little of both?

4. For an extra twist that may require a little bravery, turn out the lights and shine the black light on the mixture while stirring it.

COOL

Time for Slime-Sci

The chemical quinine—once used in tonic water to treat a mosquito-caused disease called malaria—fluoresces, or appears to glow. This means the water absorbs ultraviolet light and then emits it.

19

OOBLECK SLIME

Dr. Seuss's book *Bartholomew and the Oobleck*—a story that features sticky green glop—inspired this goo-reat creation.

☑ What You Need

- ☐ 3 cups (375 g) cornstarch
- ☐ 1 cup (237 ml) warm water
- ☐ Food coloring
- ☐ Mixing bowl
- ☐ Stirring spoon

 **Remember to keep an adult partner in slime on hand!**

How to Do It

1. Start with 2 cups (240 g) of cornstarch in the mixing bowl.

2. Add desired amount of food coloring to 1 cup (237 ml) of water. Then slowly add in with cornstarch and stir to combine. If stirred too quickly, it will seem to freeze into a solid.

3. If the mixture is too runny, add a little more cornstarch. If it's too thick, add more warm water.

4. The oobleck is done when it looks thick.

5. **Now have some fun!** Try to press it into a ball. When you stop pressing, watch the oobleck drip between your fingers as it becomes liquid again.

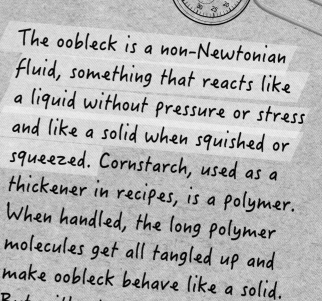

Time for Slime-Sci

The oobleck is a non-Newtonian fluid, something that reacts like a liquid without pressure or stress and like a solid when squished or squeezed. Cornstarch, used as a thickener in recipes, is a polymer. When handled, the long polymer molecules get all tangled up and make oobleck behave like a solid. But without pressure, the molecules untangle, giving us **sloppy slime**.

PHLEGM

Phlegm is like a booger somebody coughs up when sick. And this slime truly is **sick**— in the very best way!

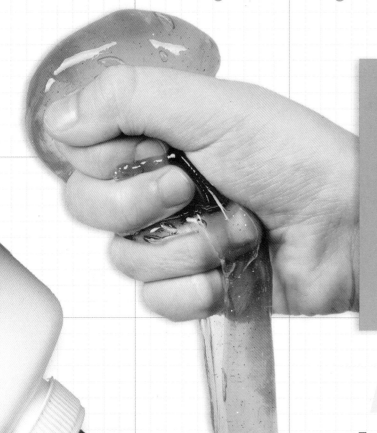

☑ What You Need

- ☐ 2 tbsp. (29.6 ml) white glue
- ☐ 1 tsp. (4.2 g) baking soda
- ☐ 1 tsp. (5 ml) contact lens solution
- ☐ Two disposable cups
- ☐ Green food coloring
- ☐ 2 tsp. (10 ml) water
- ☐ Stirring spoons
- ☐ Paper towels (optional)

How to Do It

1. Put 2 tbsp. (29.6 ml) of glue in a cup. Stir in the desired amount of food coloring.

2. In the other cup, combine 1 tsp. (4.2 g) of baking soda with 2 tsp. (10 ml) of water.

3. Pour the baking soda mixture into the glue mixture and stir well.

4. Add 1 tsp. (5 ml) of contact lens solution to the mixture. Stir well. This stuff quickly forms into a disgusting, sticky blob.

5. For an even thicker goo, press the slime between paper towels to remove the extra water.

GLUE

Time for Slime-Sci

Glue contains polyvinyl acetate, a polymer. It reacts with the baking soda to form long, X-shaped chains. The tangled polymer chains make our phlegm extra **squishy and ick.**

BRAIN SLUDGE

Milk goes well with cookies and cereal. But how does it go with vinegar? Prepare for gobs of gross fun!

How to Do It

1. Fill the cup about halfway with vinegar.

2. Fill the dropper with milk. Then put the dropper inside the cup till the tip almost touches the bottom.

3. Squeeze the dropper to release the milk into the vinegar. Watch as a cheesy white brain forms in the bottom of the cup!

4. For an extra-icky trick, pour the contents of the cup into a hand held over a sink. Behold a **shivering, quivering blob of nastiness!**

Time for Slime-Sci

Milk contains a protein called casein. The acid in the vinegar causes the casein to separate from the milk into curds. Milk curds, such as fried cheese curds, can be yummy. As for these curds, not so much!

MILK
2% Milk fat

IT'S ALIVE!

So far we've had slime that acted alive. This time our slime will be truly alive—as in **it eats, it poops, and it farts!**

What You Need

- ☐ Packet active dry yeast
- ☐ 2 small disposable cups
- ☐ 1 tsp. (4.2 g) sugar
- ☐ Lukewarm water
- ☐ Food coloring

How to Do It

1. Pour the packet of yeast into a cup.

2. Add 1 tsp. (4.2 g) of sugar.

3. Add a couple drops of food coloring to the second cup containing water. Then, add the colored water to the first cup until it is a little more than halfway full.

4. Wait about ten minutes. A disgusting froth will grow and ooze from the cup!

FART!

Time for Slime-Sci

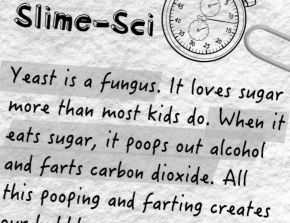

Yeast is a fungus. It loves sugar more than most kids do. When it eats sugar, it poops out alcohol and farts carbon dioxide. All this pooping and farting creates our bubbly ooze, which somehow makes bread taste delicious. If you don't have a reaction, the yeast may be old and no longer alive.

VOLCANO SLIME

Okay, so here's the thing about lava, the volcano slime found in nature: It's hot and dangerous, and it destroys everything in its path. But chill, because our slime is cool.

☑ What You Need

- ☐ Potting soil
- ☐ Two small plastic bottles with caps
- ☐ Vinegar
- ☐ Red and yellow food coloring
- ☐ 3 tbsp. (38.3 g) baking soda
- ☐ Water
- ☐ Dishwashing liquid
- ☐ Newspaper or plastic tablecloth

How to Do It

1. Fill one of the bottles halfway with vinegar. Add eight drops of yellow food coloring, and four drops of red food coloring into the bottle.

2. On a table covered with newspaper or a plastic tablecloth, build a mound of soil

around the bottle. Make sure that the bottle opening is level with the top of the mound.

3. Fill the second bottle with 3 tbsp. (38.3 g) of baking soda. Add just enough warm water to dissolve the baking soda. Then squirt some dishwashing liquid into the bottle. Put a cap over the opening, and gently shake the bottle over the sink to mix.

4. Then pour the baking soda mixture into the vinegar mixture, and **STAND BACK** as the volcano **EXPLODES!**

5. For a quick-and-easy version of this experiment, just pour some vinegar into a bottle filled about a third of the way with baking soda. **Cheap thrills!**

Time for Slime-Sci

Vinegar, as we know from a previous experiment, is an acid. Baking soda is the opposite. It's a base. When mixed, the two create carbon dioxide gas, which causes the mixture to bubble and foam. The dishwashing liquid just adds a little extra fizz.

29

FOAMY LIQUID SLIME

This slimy madness bubbles and heaves like a prop out of a horror movie. Prepare to have some **crazy-mad** fun!

☑ What You Need

- ☐ Newspaper for covering work area
- ☐ Light corn syrup
- ☐ Clear glass
- ☐ Red and blue food coloring
- ☐ Measuring spoons
- ☐ Baking soda
- ☐ Water
- ☐ Vegetable oil
- ☐ Disposable cup
- ☐ 1/4 cup (59 ml) vinegar
- ☐ Dropper

How to Do It

1. Start by covering the work area with newspaper. **This experiment can get seriously messy!**

2. Pour 1 in. (2.5 cm) of light corn syrup into the glass. Mix in several drops of red food coloring.

3. Use 1/2 teaspoon to drop piles of baking soda on top of the light corn syrup.

4. Pour water on top of the light corn syrup until it is 1 in. (2.5 cm) thick.

5. Then pour 1 in. (2.5 cm) of oil into the glass.

6. In the disposable cup, mix the vinegar with several drops of blue food coloring.

7. Using the dropper, add about half the vinegar to the glass. Watch as blue blobs form between the oil and water layers!

8. Drop more vinegar into the glass, this time near a pile of baking soda. **Watch out! This is where things get a little crazy!**

9. For even more fun, keep dropping more vinegar near the baking soda. Watch as the liquid slime becomes a freakishly foamy colorful concoction.

OIL

WATER

BAKING SODA

CORN SYRUP

Time for Slime-Sci

Our three liquids have different densities. The oil is lighter than the water and light corn syrup, so it floats on top. The vinegar can go through the oil, but it has trouble breaking through the water layer, causing it to create blue blobs. But when the vinegar meets the baking soda, carbon dioxide creates **crazy bubbly madness!**

31

FLUBBER

This goo is inspired by the 1961 Disney movie *The Absent-Minded Professor* and its 1977 remake *Flubber*, where a professor invents an out-of-control slime.

☑ What You Need

- ☐ 1 tsp. (5.7 g) Metamucil® or other powdered psyllium-based dietary supplement
- ☐ 1 cup (237 ml) water
- ☐ Food coloring
- ☐ Large microwave-safe bowl
- ☐ Oven mitts
- ☐ Large plate or cookie sheet
- ☐ Plastic spoon
- ☐ Ice cube tray (optional)

How to Do It

1. Mix the Metamucil® and water in the large bowl.

2. Stir in two to three drops of food coloring.

3. Using a partner in slime's help, put the bowl in the microwave on high for two minutes. **Watch to make sure the flubber doesn't bubble over the edge of the bowl.**

4. Have the adult remove the bowl from the microwave while wearing oven mitts.

5. Let the slime cool. Then repeat Steps 3 and 4. The flubber gets thicker as it cools and becomes more rubbery each time it's cooked.

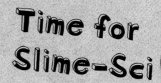

Time for Slime-Sci

Psyllium, a plant fiber, and water thicken when heated. The more they're heated, the thicker they get. Psyllium absorbs all the water, creating goo that won't stick to fingers.

6. When the flubber has reached the right consistency (usually after five to six microwavings), have an adult partner in slime pour it onto the plate or cookie sheet.

7. Spread it out using the spoon, and let it cool.

8. To shape the slime, pour warm flubber into an ice tray and let it cool.

READY FOR PRIME SLIME

Ever see someone get slimed on TV? Well, it's time to create what's in that bucket and celebrate with a **slimefest!**

What You Need

- ☐ 2 packets green Jell-O®
- ☐ 8 cups (1 kg) of flour
- ☐ 4 cups (.95 l) water
- ☐ 1 cup (237 ml) baby shampoo
- ☐ Green food coloring
- ☐ Large bucket
- ☐ Whisk
- ☐ Plastic spoon

Before engaging in a *slime-slinging slimefest*, make sure no one reacts to—or is allergic to—wheat flour or food coloring. Friends may let friends get ick, but friends don't let friends get sick!

How to Do It

1. Combine the Jell-O® and half the flour in the bucket. Mix the ingredients with a whisk.

2. Add the water, and stir everything together with a whisk until smooth.

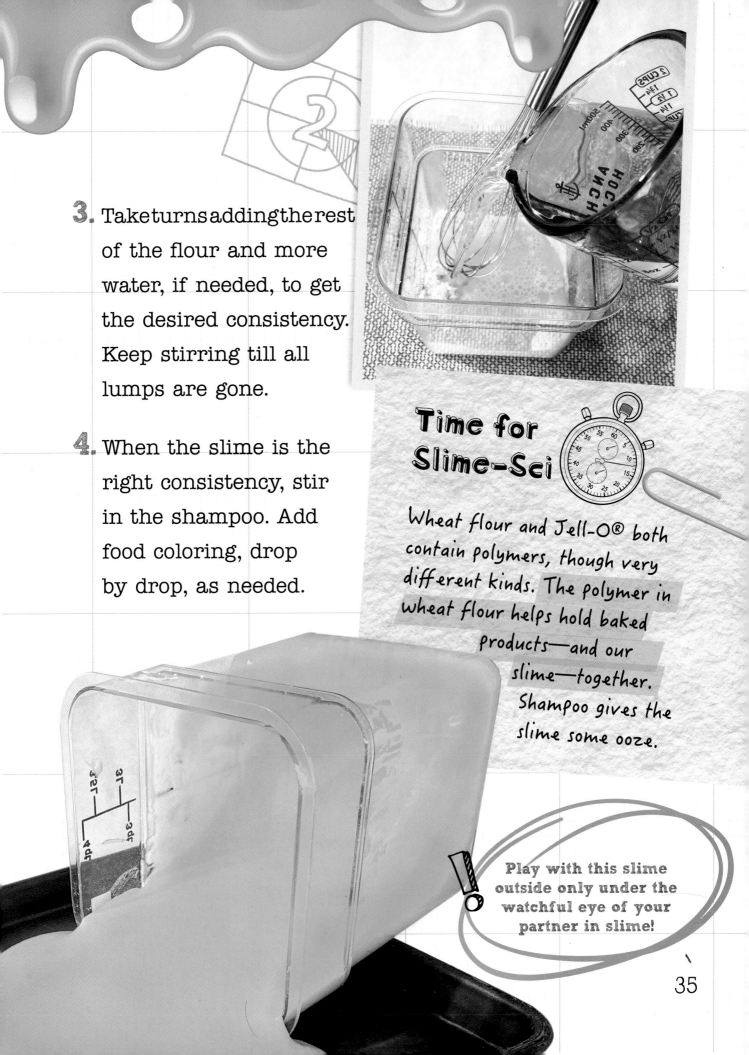

3. Take turns adding the rest of the flour and more water, if needed, to get the desired consistency. Keep stirring till all lumps are gone.

4. When the slime is the right consistency, stir in the shampoo. Add food coloring, drop by drop, as needed.

Time for Slime-Sci

Wheat flour and Jell-O® both contain polymers, though very different kinds. The polymer in wheat flour helps hold baked products—and our slime—together. Shampoo gives the slime some ooze.

Play with this slime outside only under the watchful eye of your partner in slime!

SHOCKING ELECTRO SLIME

Get ready for some shocking results as electricity causes slime to change shape or size!

☑ What You Need

- ☐ 3/4 cup (90 g) cornstarch
- ☐ 2 cups (474 ml) vegetable oil
- ☐ Large bowl
- ☐ Plastic spoon
- ☐ Inflated balloon

How to Do It

1. Mix the cornstarch and the oil together in the bowl.

2. Rub the balloon against dry hair.

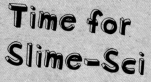

3. Then hold the balloon close to a spoonful of slime as it drips from the spoon. Watch the slime gravitate toward the electrical charge on the balloon!

Time for Slime-Sci

This slime contains electroactive polymers. It gets an electrical charge from being rubbed on hair. This will cause it to attract the cornstarch mixture—but only when it's dripping. Holding the balloon over the bowl won't achieve the same results because the gravity of the big blob is stronger than its electrical charge.

GLUE-Y SLIME

Let's make disgusting fun with greasy, grimy, gopher-gutty goo!!

☑ **What You Need**

- ☐ White glue
- ☐ Green food coloring
- ☐ Two disposable cups
- ☐ Spoon for stirring
- ☐ Liquid laundry starch

How to Do It

1. Combine a big glob of white glue with a few drops of food coloring in one of the disposable cups.

2. Fill the second cup halfway with laundry starch.

3. Drizzle the glue mixture into the starch. Rotate the starch cup as you drizzle the glue into it so the glue doesn't land in one place.

4. Now reach in and grab a handful of your slippery, stringy, glue-y goo. **Gross—but fun!**

This slime is safe to handle, but wash hands afterward!

Time for Slime-Sci

Molecules in the starch connect with glue molecules to make long, tough, stringy strands. Those stringy strands of slime demonstrate the cross-linking power of polymers.

FLUFFIEST SLIME

A pet dog or cat is most people's favorite ball of fluff. But this slime takes fluff to a whole new level!

☑ What You Need

- ☐ 1/2 cup (120 ml) white glue
- ☐ 3 cups (720 ml) foaming shaving cream
- ☐ 1/8 cup (30 ml) foaming hand soap
- ☐ Blue and green food coloring
- ☐ 1/8 cup (30 ml) liquid starch
- ☐ Mixing bowl
- ☐ Spoon for stirring
- ☐ Measuring cups
- ☐ Measuring spoons

How to Do It

1. Combine the glue, shaving cream, and hand soap in the bowl. Stir well.

2. Add food coloring, and stir some more. Shaving cream absorbs food coloring, so you may need to add more.

3. Slowly stir in the liquid starch **1 tbsp. (15 ml) at a time.** Stir until the slime pulls away from the sides of the bowl.

4. Knead the slime with bare hands. If the slime is sticky, add 1 tbsp. (15 ml) of liquid starch at a time. But be careful: **Too much starch can put the tough in fluff.**

Time for Slime-Sci

The molecules in the glue and starch create long polymer chains like what we see in flexible plastic. Those chains allow this slime to stretch and bounce. The shaving cream gives our slime its fluff.

BUTTER SLIME

This slime looks like butter. It even spreads like butter. Even though it's not edible, it's fun to pretend to play with food!

☑ What You Need

- ☐ 1 cup (240 ml) white glue
- ☐ 2 tsp. (10 ml) body lotion
- ☐ 1 tsp. (5 ml) baby oil
- ☐ Yellow food coloring
- ☐ 2 tsp. (10 g) baking soda
- ☐ 2 cups (240 g) cornstarch
- ☐ 1-3 tsp. (5-15 ml) contact lens solution
- ☐ Mixing bowl
- ☐ Spoon for stirring
- ☐ Measuring cups
- ☐ Measuring spoons

How to Do It

1. Combine baking soda and cornstarch in the mixing bowl.

2. Add glue, body lotion, baby oil, and food coloring. Stir to combine.

3. Add 1 tsp. (5 ml) contact lens solution, and stir some more. Add more contact lens solution 1 tsp. (5 ml) at a time if the slime sticks to your hands.

4. When the slime pulls away from the sides of the bowl, knead it in your hands.

Time for Slime-Sci

Glue molecules form chains with a type of salt called borate in the contact lens solution and the polymers in cornstarch. This gives our slime its smooth, stretchable texture.

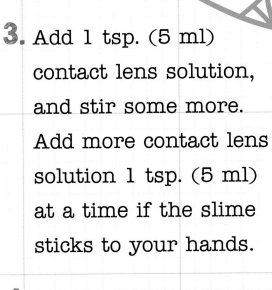

SOFTEST SLIME

This soft-serve slime will be hard to resist! Prepare for hours of stretchy, gooey fun!

☑ What You Need

- ☐ 1/2 cup (120 ml) white glue
- ☐ 1/2 cup (120 ml) foaming shaving cream
- ☐ 2 tsp. (10 ml) lotion
- ☐ 1/3 cup (40 g) cornstarch
- ☐ 1/3 cup (40 g) baby powder
- ☐ 1/8 cup (30 ml) contact lens solution
- ☐ Mixing bowl
- ☐ Spoon for stirring
- ☐ Measuring cups
- ☐ Measuring spoons
- ☐ Food coloring (optional)

How to Do It

1. Combine cornstarch and baby powder in the mixing bowl.

2. Add glue, foaming shaving cream, lotion, and food coloring, if using. Stir to combine.

3. Very slowly pour the contact lens solution into the mixture just 1 tsp. (5 ml) at a time. Only use as much as you need to avoid making the slime tough. Keep stirring till the slime pulls away from the bowl.

4. Knead the slime in your hands.

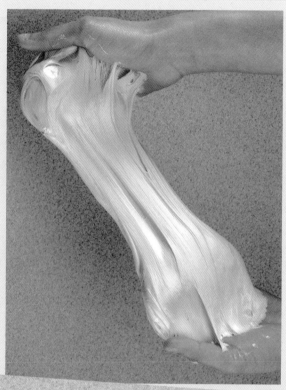

Lotion makes the slime soft!

Time for Slime-Sci

As with our buttery slime, the glue molecules form strong chains with the borate in the contact lens solution, as well as with the cornstarch. The lotion and shaving cream make the slime soft, while the baby powder helps it release from the bowl.

STICKY GLUE SCIENCE

We've barely touched the sticky surface about how glue makes for good goo. Let's fix that.

Our past few experiments used white glue combined with contact lens solution or some starchy powder. Glue is a polymer containing long chains of polyvinyl acetate. These chains easily slide past one another—kind of like slippery spaghetti noodles on a plate.

That slip-sliding texture helps glue pour easily from the bottle.

It may seem logical to assume glue is sticky because of sticky polymers.

WRONG!

GLUE

Glue gets its runny texture from the slippery polyvinyl acetate molecules within it.

But that changes when we add starch or contact lens solution. (Think baking soda, laundry starch, or cornstarch.) As the borate ions—molecules with electrical charges—combine with glue, they help the polymer molecules develop sticky superpowers.

As the mixture forms, it now takes a lot of energy to break the new bonds. The chemical changes can even make the mixture feel cool to the touch. That reaction is what gives us our **wonderfully weird** non-Newtonian glue-based goo.

The combination of contact lens solution and baking soda is similar in chemical makeup to laundry detergent.

NEW BRAND CLEANER

DELVING DEEPER INTO SLIME

Slime is everywhere, and it turns out to be pretty useful.

Opossums spray **stinky slime** from their butts to protect them from predators, animals that otherwise would want to hunt them.

Our bodies are full of the slime called mucus. Mucus helps us swallow. It lines our stomachs and protects them from damage. It filters the air as we breathe it. When it pours out of our noses, it rids our bodies of stuff that makes us sick. Scientists believe our noses produce between **1 and 2 quarts (.95 to 1.9 l) of snot** each day.

Scientists believe snot—**everyone's favorite slime**—helps dolphins communicate with one another using clicks.

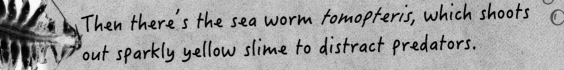

Then there's the sea worm *tomopteris*, which shoots out sparkly yellow slime to distract predators.